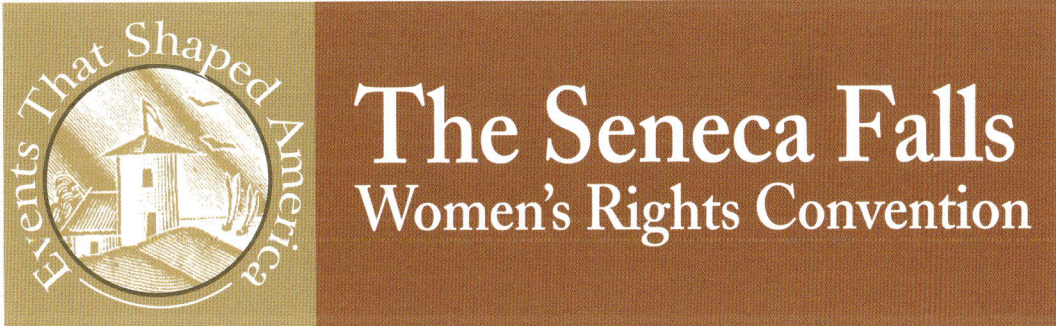

The Seneca Falls Women's Rights Convention

Sabrina Crewe and Dale Anderson

South Huntington Pub. Lib.
145 Pidgeon Hill Rd.
Huntington Sta., N.Y. 11746

Gareth Stevens Publishing
A WORLD ALMANAC EDUCATION GROUP COMPANY

Please visit our web site at: www.garethstevens.com
For a free color catalog describing Gareth Stevens Publishing's list of high-quality books and multimedia programs, call 1-800-542-2595 (USA) or 1-800-387-3178 (Canada). Gareth Stevens Publishing's fax: (414) 332-3567.

Library of Congress Cataloging-in-Publication Data

Crewe, Sabrina.
    The Seneca Falls Women's Rights Convention / by Sabrina Crewe and Dale Anderson.
       p. cm. — (Events that shaped America)
    Includes bibliographical references and index.
    ISBN 0-8368-3408-9 (lib. bdg.)
    1. Woman's Rights Convention (1st: 1848: Seneca Falls, N.Y.)—Juvenile literature.
    2. Women's rights—United States—History—Juvenile literature. 3. Feminists—United States—Biography—Juvenile literature. I. Anderson, Dale, 1953- . II. Title.
III. Series.
HQ1418.C75   2004
305.42'0973—dc22   2004045267

This North American edition first published in 2005 by
Gareth Stevens Publishing
A World Almanac Education Group Company
330 West Olive Street, Suite 100
Milwaukee, WI 53212 USA

This edition © 2005 by Gareth Stevens Publishing.

Produced by Discovery Books
Editor: Sabrina Crewe
Designer and page production: Sabine Beaupré
Photo researcher: Sabrina Crewe
Maps and diagrams: Stefan Chabluk
Gareth Stevens editor: Jim Mezzanotte
Gareth Stevens art direction: Tammy West
Gareth Stevens production: Jessica Morris

Photo credits: Corbis: cover, pp. 5, 6, 8, 9, 11, 12, 13, 17, 19, 20, 22, 23, 24, 25, 27; The Granger Collection: pp. 18; National Park Service, Women's Rights National Historical Park: pp. 14, 16, 21, 26; North Wind Picture Archives: pp. 4, 7, 10; Seneca Falls Historical Society: p. 15.

All rights reserved. No part of this book may be reproduced, stored in a retrieval system, or transmitted in any form or by any means, electronic, mechanical, photocopying, recording, or otherwise, without the prior written permission of the copyright holder.

Printed in the United States of America

1 2 3 4 5 6 7 8 9 09 08 07 06 05 04

Contents

Introduction 4
Chapter 1: New Ideas 6
Chapter 2: Planning a Meeting 14
Chapter 3: At Seneca Falls 16
Chapter 4: Fighting for Equality 22
Conclusion 26
Time Line 28
Things to Think About and Do 29
Glossary 30
Further Information 31
Index 32

Introduction

More than fifty years after the Seneca Falls Convention, women were still trying to get equal rights. **Suffragettes** march in New York City in this 1911 photo.

Meeting in Seneca Falls

On July 19 and 20, 1848, about three hundred people gathered for a **convention** in the small New York town of Seneca Falls. At the meeting, these people—most of whom were women—discussed the fact that American women did not have the same rights as American men. They discussed how husbands could take their wives' property and any money they earned. They talked about how women were denied schooling, the chance to enter many jobs, and voting rights.

A Declaration

At the convention, a document called the "Declaration of **Sentiments**" was presented. Like the Declaration of

Independence, it laid out injustices and said it was time for a change.

Starting a Revolution

The Seneca Falls Convention and the "Declaration of Sentiments" did not seem very important at the time. The convention, however, launched a **revolution**. This revolution was not a sudden event, but a change that took place over many years. After 1848, the role of women slowly began to change, and the long struggle for equal rights began.

Many generations of women joined in that struggle. They battled the leaders and laws of the United States. They wrote and spoke and shouted and marched and went to prison in their efforts to make men change their views. They finally succeeded, in 1920—more than seventy years after the Seneca Falls Convention—when women got the right to vote.

Two Declarations

"We hold these truths to be self-evident, that all men are created equal, that they are endowed by their Creator with certain unalienable Rights, that among these, are Life, Liberty, and the pursuit of Happiness."

Second paragraph of the Declaration of Independence, Second Continental Congress, 1776

"We hold these truths to be self-evident; that all men and women are created equal; that they are endowed by their Creator with certain unalienable rights; that among these, are life, liberty, and the pursuit of happiness; . . ."

Second paragraph of the "Declaration of Sentiments," Seneca Falls Convention, 1848

In 1920, these women and many others celebrated their right to vote with a parade.

Chapter One
New Ideas

Women in the United States

When Americans signed the Declaration of Independence in 1776 and founded their own nation, they did so because they believed they were being denied their rights and freedoms under British rule. But in the newly formed United States, the rights of women did not improve at all.

Women had few rights. Before marriage, they had to obey their fathers. Afterward, they had to obey their husbands. Wives could not sign contracts or write wills unless their husbands allowed it. They could not enter most professions. The great majority could not vote—only in New Jersey did women have that right, and in 1807 it was taken away.

A Woman's Role

Running the household and raising children were a woman's main tasks. Women had to grow and make most foods from scratch. They had to do laundry by hand and carry water to the house so they could cook and clean. Ready-made goods

In the 1700s, men took charge of everything except household duties.

Lowell Girls

Lowell, Massachusetts, became a major center of the growing U.S. **textile** industry in the 1820s. Its factories were staffed by women aged fifteen to twenty-five years old. The factory owners had strict rules for these "Lowell Girls." Employees had to work for at least a year, live in company-run boardinghouses, and go to church every week. The girls worked twelve to fourteen hours a day on weekdays and half as much on Saturday. If workers protested the long hours and the pay cuts that sometimes happened, the factory owners squashed the protests. Despite all the hardships, women continued to work at the Lowell factories into the early 1900s.

Lowell Girls working the looms in the 1850s.

were not widely available, so women had to make their own soap, candles, clothes, and quilts. All these tasks took huge amounts of time and energy.

Running the household was a full-time job, but most women did far more. Farm women labored in the fields. Others worked at night, sewing gloves or clothing to earn a little extra money for the family. Women helped out at family-owned stores and ran boardinghouses. The growth of factories in the 1800s drew many women into manufacturing work outside the home.

A great reformer, Dorothea Dix helped improve conditions in prisons and institutions for mentally ill people.

The Ideal Woman

In the early 1800s, people believed there were three characteristics that women should show. Ideal women were thought to be more religious than men and so should have better morals; they were expected to maintain orderly homes; and they were supposed to obey their husbands. These beliefs strongly shaped the way women were viewed.

Calls for Change

Starting in the 1820s, many Americans began to push for changes that were based on new ideas about helping people and improving society. Several **reform** movements arose, each aimed at fixing a particular social problem. Many **reformers** were women, and it was in this role that women first learned they could have some influence in the world outside their own homes.

Subordination

"It is needful that certain relations be sustained, which involve the duties of **subordination**.... [These include] husband and wife.... The superior... is to direct, and the inferior is to yield obedience. Society could never go forward... unless these superior and subordinate relations be instituted and sustained."

Catherine Beecher, A Treatise on Domestic Economy, *1842*

The Temperance Movement

The anti-alcohol, or **temperance**, movement was one of the first reform efforts of the 1800s. Its goal was to convince people to drink less alcohol because reformers believed that drinking caused most problems in the family.

Temperance, like many reform movements of the period, was greatly influenced by religion. The reformers complained about "Demon Rum" and compared alcohol to the devil. Heavy drinkers were seen as sinners whose souls would be saved if they could be convinced not to drink. Women played major roles in thousands of temperance groups that formed across the nation.

A woman attacks a bottle-shaped cannon labeled "Rum" in an anti-alcohol poster.

The temperance movement continued into the 1900s. Eventually, it won a huge victory when a 1919 **amendment** outlawed making or selling alcohol in the United States. The ban lasted just over ten years before it was **repealed**.

The Need for Schooling

"If we do not prepare children to become good citizens—if we do not develop their capacities, if we do not enrich their minds with knowledge, imbue their hearts with the love of truth and duty, and a reverence for all things sacred and holy, then our republic must go down to destruction."

Horace Mann, annual report on education in Massachusetts, 1845

Helping the Unfortunate

Some reformers aimed to help people who suffered from hardships. In the early 1800s, schools for the deaf and blind were founded. People began to set up orphanages.

Schools for Everyone

Another area of change was in education. The efforts of reformer Horace Mann led to the spread of public schools and more spending on education.

Some women reformers pushed hard to make sure that girls got an education. Several founded high schools for girls. In 1837, Mary Lyon opened a new school in Massachusetts that educated women to an even higher level. It became Mount Holyoke College, the first women's college in the United States.

The founding of public schools, such as the one shown here, meant the beginning of widespread education for children whose families were too poor to pay for private schooling.

Freeing the Slaves

The most important reform movement of the 1800s was the **abolition** movement, which fought to get rid of slavery. Slaves had no rights: Owners controlled every aspect of a slave's life and work. Families were split up when slaveowners sold spouses or children to other plantations, causing much heartbreak. Slaves who did not obey orders were beaten, and those who were caught trying to escape were often killed.

Women in the Abolition Movement

Many antislavery workers, or abolitionists, were women. Some were African Americans, including those who had been born free in the North and others who had been born to slavery and escaped.

By 1840, about half the people working in the abolition movement were women. Although men still led most reform movements, women had found a voice in their campaigns for temperance and against slavery. Soon, they would use that voice to demand rights for themselves.

This scene of a slave child being taken from his mother is from a famous book, *Uncle Tom's Cabin*, written by Harriet Beecher Stowe and published in 1852. The novel let Americans know about the horrors of slavery.

Lucretia Coffin Mott (1793–1880)

Lucretia Coffin was born into a **Quaker** family in Nantucket, Massachusetts. Her parents sent her to a Quaker school, and she stayed on there to become an assistant teacher. After she married James Mott, Lucretia Coffin Mott lived in Philadelphia and became very involved in various reform movements. The Motts were active abolitionists, and they made their home a safe house for African Americans who fled from slavery.

Lucretia Mott was also a well-known lecturer about temperance and the rights of working people. And in 1848, with the Seneca Falls Convention, she took up yet another cause: women's rights. In 1866, Mott was chosen as the first president of the Equal Rights Association. She gave her last public address on the thirtieth anniversary of the Seneca Falls Convention, when she was eighty-five years old.

A Meeting in London

In 1840, the antislavery movement held an international conference in London, England. Among the Americans who attended were Elizabeth Cady Stanton and Lucretia Coffin Mott. Women were not allowed to take part in the meeting—not even Mott, a prominent abolitionist. Like Elizabeth Stanton, she was forced to sit in the gallery and watch.

The two women decided that they should hold a meeting in the United States to discuss the lack of freedom and rights for women. It would be several years, however, before Stanton and Mott acted on their idea. In the meantime, Mott continued her antislavery work in Philadelphia, and Stanton began to raise a family in Boston.

Elizabeth Cady Stanton had seven children, but she didn't believe women should be just wives and mothers. After 1848, she spent her life trying to gain equality for women.

About Time

"As the convention adjourned, the remark was heard on all sides, 'It is about time some demand was made for new liberties for women.' As Mrs. Mott and I walked home, arm in arm, . . . we resolved to hold a convention as soon as we returned home, and form a society to advocate the rights of women."

Elizabeth Cady Stanton, Eighty Years and More, *1898*

Chapter Two
Planning a Meeting

Elizabeth Stanton and her family lived in this house in Seneca Falls in 1848. It is preserved as part of the Women's Rights National Historical Park.

Moving to Seneca Falls

In 1847, the Stantons moved to Seneca Falls in New York, where Elizabeth Stanton soon became deeply unhappy. She spent her days looking after her children and running a household without help from her husband.

Elizabeth Cady Stanton (1815–1902)

Born in Johnstown, New York, in 1815, Elizabeth Cady was taught at home and later sent to a girl's academy in Troy, New York. A few years after graduating, while a teacher, Cady met Henry Brewster Stanton, a lawyer and antislavery crusader, whom she married in 1840.

After the Seneca Falls Convention, the movement for women's rights became Elizabeth Cady Stanton's life's work. Stanton was president of the National Woman **Suffrage** Association (1869–1890) and the National American Woman Suffrage Association (1890–1892). The day before she died, at the age of eighty-seven, she wrote a letter to President Theodore Roosevelt, urging him to support women's suffrage.

The map (left) shows Seneca Falls and the neighboring town of Waterloo where the convention planners first met.

The only advertising for the convention was a small notice (below) in the *Seneca County Courier* a few days before.

In the summer of 1848, Lucretia Mott came to nearby Waterloo to visit her sister. On July 13, Elizabeth Stanton went to tea at the house of Jane Hunt in Waterloo. Mott, her sister Martha Coffin Wright, and a neighbor named Mary Ann M'Clintock were also there. Stanton told them how unhappy she was with the lack of equality in her life.

A Decision is Made

That day, the five women decided they would hold a meeting at which women could discuss the injustices they suffered and talk about how to begin a campaign for equal rights. They chose a nearby chapel where the meeting would be held and wrote an advertisement to announce the event in a local newspaper.

On July 16, the five women got together again at Mary Ann M'Clintock's house in Waterloo and planned some more. They decided to draft a declaration to offer at the meeting. While all helped write the piece, it was mostly Stanton's work.

Women's Rights Convention.

A Convention to discuss the social, civil and religious condition and rights of Woman, will be held in the Wesleyan Chapel, at Seneca Falls, N. Y., on Wednesday and Thursday the 19th and 20th of July current, commencing at 10 o'clock A. M.

During the first day, the meeting will be exclusively for Women, which all are earnestly invited to attend. The public generally are invited to be present on the second day, when LUCRETIA MOTT, of Philadelphia, and others both ladies and gentlemen, will address the Convention.

Chapter Three

At Seneca Falls

Arriving at the Meeting

The Seneca Falls Convention was held less than a week later. On July 19, 1848, when the organizers reached the Wesleyan Chapel in Seneca Falls, where the meeting was to be held, they found that they did not have the key to unlock the door. The young nephew of one organizer had to climb through an open window and open the door from inside.

People came from several miles around. Charlotte Woodward, nineteen years old, came from her family's farm nearby. She later recalled that each time she reached a crossroads, more wagons and carriages joined the group traveling to the town until "we were a procession."

The remains of the Wesleyan Methodist Chapel stand under a protective structure in Seneca Falls today. In the years after 1848, the building served as an opera hall, a movie theater, a car dealership, and a laundromat.

Frederick Douglass (c.1817–1895)

Frederick Douglass was born into slavery in Maryland, but in 1838 he managed to escape to New York. In 1841, Douglass got up at an anti-slavery meeting and told the crowd what slavery was like. From then on, Douglass became celebrated as a speaker in the abolition movement. In the 1840s, he purchased his freedom and began publishing an abolitionist newspaper, the *North Star*. After the Civil War freed black people from slavery, Douglass worked for the U.S. government and continued to speak in favor of equality for women.

The Men

Although men were not supposed to attend the first day, about forty showed up. They included Lucretia Mott's husband James, Jane Hunt's husband Richard, and the abolitionist Frederick Douglass. The women agreed to let the men in.

Elizabeth Stanton's husband Henry did not come. He had objected strongly to one of the **resolutions** being presented, which said women should have the right to vote. Henry Stanton told his wife he would leave town if she insisted on keeping the resolution. Elizabeth Stanton kept it anyway, and so her husband left.

Oppression on All Sides

"Having deprived her of this first right as a citizen, the elective **franchise**, thereby leaving her without representation in the halls of legislation, he has oppressed her on all sides."

From the "Declaration of Sentiments," 1848

This print depicting the convention shows Elizabeth Cady Stanton standing on the stage to address the audience.

The Meeting Begins

In spite of the fact that the women were gathering to assert their rights, it was not thought that women could lead a meeting! James Mott was chosen to chair the convention, and Mary Ann M'Clintock served as secretary.

Lucretia Mott gave the first speech on the first day of the convention. An experienced speaker, she laid out the objectives of the meeting. She described the many ways in which women suffered from their lack of rights.

The "Declaration of Sentiments"

Other speakers followed, and then Stanton rose to give the first speech of her life—the first of many, it would turn out. Nervous at first, she soon found her voice. Stanton began by reading the "Declaration of Sentiments."

The declaration listed **grievances** against men. These included denying women the right to vote, making husbands the masters of their wives' property, preventing divorce, withholding education, and blocking women from entering various careers.

Signing the Declaration

The next morning, on July 20, 1848, the meeting assembled again. The "Declaration of Sentiments" was read once more and approved overwhelmingly. Sixty-eight women agreed to sign the document. Thirty-two men also signed, stating that they were "in favor of the movement."

The resolutions were then all agreed to, except one. Deciding on whether to demand suffrage was very difficult. Like Henry Stanton, Lucretia Mott had warned Elizabeth Stanton before the meeting to drop this demand, saying Stanton would "make the whole convention ridiculous." But Stanton held firm.

Amelia Bloomer was a reformer best known for encouraging women to wear shorter skirts with long undergarments now known as "bloomers." She came to the meeting but would not sign the "Declaration of Sentiments" because she thought it was too **radical**.

The Resolutions

Stanton had drafted several resolutions that spelled out the changes that the women wanted. On the first day of the meeting, she read them aloud for the participants to consider. The resolutions included the following:

Women and men should have equal rights.
Laws that limit women's rights are invalid.
Women should be given an education.
Women should have the right to speak and teach in churches.
Men should have the same punishments as women for moral offenses.
Women should have the right to vote.

A cartoon, published after the Seneca Falls meeting, pokes fun at the speakers and the audience.

The Demand for Suffrage Is Approved

At the meeting on July 20, Stanton spoke forcefully in favor of the right to vote. Frederick Douglass rose from the audience to add his arguments to hers. With a slim majority, the convention agreed to demand suffrage for women.

That evening, the meeting came together one last time. Mott introduced a new resolution calling for women to have the chance to pursue whatever careers they wanted, and it was approved. Mary Ann M'Clintock and Douglass then gave short speeches urging the women to act. Mott then spoke a last time, for an hour, and the meeting was closed.

The Public Response

Word about the Seneca Falls meeting spread quickly. Most newspapers were hostile to the women's call for change and harshly attacked the convention. They belittled women's need for legal rights and scorned their ideas for equality.

A Vote for Justice
"If that government only is just which governs by the free consent of the governed, there can be no reason in the world for denying to woman the exercise of the elective franchise."

Frederick Douglass, the North Star, *1848*

The criticism was so harsh that some of the people who had signed the "Declaration of Sentiments" later asked that their names be taken off it. The outcry had a benefit, however, because it gave the convention huge publicity. Stanton cheerfully pointed this out in a letter to a friend: "There is no danger of the Woman Question dying for want of notice. Every paper you take up has something to say about it."

A Shocking Incident

"This [convention] is the most shocking and unnatural incident ever recorded in the history of womanity. If our ladies will insist on voting and legislating, where, gentlemen, will be our dinners . . . ? Where our domestic firesides and the holes in our stockings?"

Oneida Whig *newspaper, New York, August 1, 1848*

The "Declaration of Sentiments" inspired generations of women in their long struggle for equality. Its words are etched into this memorial wall in the Women's Rights National Historical Park in Seneca Falls.

Chapter Four

Fighting for Equality

A Slow Start

After Seneca Falls, the movement for women's rights grew slowly. One reason for the slow growth was that many reformers were busy with the antislavery movement, which became a major focus in the 1850s and early 1860s. Another reason was that women's rights workers had too many different goals. They wanted property rights and the right to control wages. They worked for better divorce laws and more opportunities in education and careers. All of these goals meant the movement lacked a clear focus.

Over the years, women continued to campaign for the vote. They marched, they lobbied politicians, and they published posters such as this one, appealing to the common sense of the public.

Women in Chains
"Women are in chains, and their servitude is all the more debasing because they do not realize it. O, to compel them to see and feel, and to give them the courage and conscience to speak and act for their own freedom, though they face the scorn and contempt of all the world for doing it!"

Susan B. Anthony, 1870

A New Partner for Stanton

Elizabeth Stanton had been working for equality for a few years when she met Susan B. Anthony in 1851. They were perfect partners. Stanton could inspire crowds and had bold ideas. Anthony was a great organizer—she tirelessly recruited workers and concentrated on getting the movement's message out to the world. Together, the two became leaders of the early women's rights movement. In 1869, Stanton and Anthony formed the National Woman Suffrage Association. Their aim was to win not only the right to vote, but also a broad range of other rights, such as an eight-hour workday and equal wages.

The partnership of Elizabeth Stanton (left) and Susan B. Anthony (right) lasted for many decades. Neither lived long enough to see women gain suffrage in 1920, but they achieved a great deal for women's rights.

Losses and Gains

Between 1870 and 1910, women in more than thirty states tried to win the right to vote. These efforts all failed.

There were some gains, however. In 1869–1870, the **U.S. territories** of Wyoming and Utah gave women the vote, a right that continued in the 1890s, when the territories became states. Colorado and Idaho also gave suffrage to women in the 1890s.

Their Rights and Nothing Less

"Principle, Not Policy. Justice, Not Favors—Men, Their Rights and Nothing More. Women, Their Rights and Nothing Less."

Susan B. Anthony, slogan for the Revolution, *a women's rights newspaper, 1868*

By the 1900s, new generations of suffragettes had joined the cause. Young and old, they battled for equality in the face of opposition. This cartoon, published in 1915, shows a shocked father discovering his daughter is a suffragette.

Lifetimes of Effort

"Hundreds of women gave the accumulated possibilities of an entire lifetime, thousands gave years of their lives. . . . It was a continuous, seemingly endless, chain of activity. Young suffragists who helped forge the last links of that chain were not born when it began. Old suffragists who forged the first links were dead when it ended."

Carrie Chapman Catt and Nettie Rogers Shuter, Woman Suffrage and Politics, *1923*

The Nineteenth Amendment

After 1900, the suffrage campaign gained steam under new leaders such as Alice Paul and Carrie Chapman Catt. It was the age of the suffragette, and mass marches took place across the country to call attention to the cause of women's rights.

Starting in 1912, several more states agreed to give women the vote. Finally, in 1919, Congress approved the Nineteenth Amendment to the U.S. Constitution, granting women the right to vote across the country.

Ratifying the Nineteenth Amendment

Most states quickly passed the Nineteenth Amendment. After thirty-five state **legislatures** had **ratified** the amendment, one more was needed for it to become law. National attention focused on Tennessee, the next state to vote. In 1920, Tennessee legislator Harry Burn cast the deciding vote in favor of national suffrage. In his pocket, he carried a letter from his mother urging him to approve the amendment.

A Vote At Last

The Nineteenth Amendment was declared ratified on August 26, 1920. It had been seventy-two years since the meeting at Seneca Falls. Stanton, Mott, and the other organizers of the meeting had all died. So had the women who had signed the "Declaration of Sentiments"—all but one. Charlotte Woodward, nineteen years old back in 1848, was ninety-one years old in 1920. That year, she cast a vote in the presidential election.

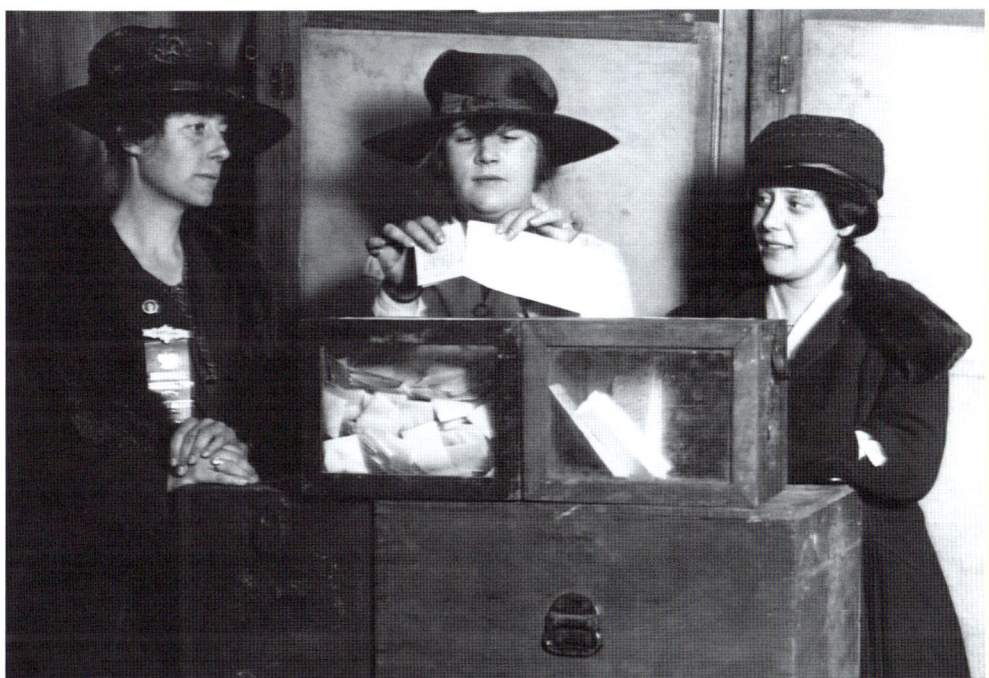

Three women vote at a polling station in New York City. In 1920, women voted for the first time in a presidential election.

Conclusion

The decision to hold a women's rights convention took place in Jane Hunt's house in the village of Waterloo, New York. It is now part of the Women's Rights National Historical Park.

Visiting Seneca Falls

The Wesleyan Chapel in Seneca Falls, New York, is part of the Women's Rights National Historical Park, and the remaining parts of the building have been preserved in a protective structure. Visitors to the historical park can visit the chapel, tour Elizabeth Cady Stanton's house nearby, and see Jane Hunt's house in neighboring Waterloo.

Women Today

Several generations of women have grown up taking basic rights and freedoms for granted. Women in the United States would be amazed if anyone questioned their right to be educated, to own property, to express an opinion, or to work. But these everyday rights were just dreams to the women at

Seneca Falls. The gains that women have made—and now hardly think about—can be traced back to that meeting in 1848. The people who spoke there laid the groundwork for the idea that all men *and women* are created equal.

In the early 2000s, women enjoy many of the rights demanded at the Seneca Falls Convention. They have made the greatest advances in education. By 2000, more than half of the people graduating from U.S. colleges were women.

In the Workplace

Women have also entered many careers once closed to them, from firefighting and space exploration to professional sports and corporate business. Yet women still suffer from **discrimination** in the working world. In 2000, they earned only 73 cents for each dollar earned by men. Not very many women have found jobs in the highest management ranks. Clearly, women are still trying to gain complete equality with men.

Employment Monopolized
"He has monopolized nearly all the profitable employments, and from those she is permitted to follow, she receives but a scanty remuneration."

From the "Declaration of Sentiments," 1848

In 2000, Condoleezza Rice was chosen by President-elect George W. Bush to be U.S. National Security Advisor. She is one of few American women to rise high in the nation's leadership.

Time Line

1783 New Jersey state constitution gives women the right to vote.
1807 Women in New Jersey lose the right to vote.
1833 American Anti-Slavery Society is founded.
1837 Mary Lyon opens first women's college, in Massachusetts.
1840 Elizabeth Cady Stanton and Lucretia Coffin Mott meet at London antislavery conference.
1848 July 13: Stanton, Mott, and others decide to hold convention in Seneca Falls.
July 14: Advertisement for convention appears in local newspaper.
July 16: "Declaration of Sentiments" is drafted.
July 19–20: Seneca Falls Convention takes place, and "Declaration of Sentiments" and resolutions are approved.
1851 Stanton meets Susan B. Anthony.
1869 National Woman Suffrage Association (NWSA) and American Woman Suffrage Association (AWSA) are founded.
Wyoming Territory gives women the vote.
1870 Utah Territory gives women the vote.
1890 NWSA and AWSA join to form National American Woman Suffrage Association.
1919 Prohibition begins, banning the making and selling of alcohol. Congress approves Nineteenth Amendment.
1920 August 26: Nineteenth Amendment is declared ratified, and women gain the right to vote.

Things to Think About and Do

Before and After
Find out what you can about life for girls in the 1800s, before the women's movement brought equality and new ways of thinking. Think about the life of girls among your friends and family today. List the differences between then and now. What do you think are the most important changes?

A Reform Movement
Think of something in your community today that may benefit from reforms of the kind that were made in the 1800s. The reforms could have to do with school, the environment, or a safety issue. Decide what you think should be done and how you would start a campaign for reform.

A Declaration
Imagine you are a member of a group in society that for some reason lacks the rights of other people. Find a copy of the Declaration of Independence and use it to help you write a declaration of rights for your group. Explain your grievances —what is wrong with your situation now—and make a list of resolutions for changes that would help give your group equal rights.

Glossary

abolition: getting rid of something, especially slavery.

amendment: official change or addition made to the United States Constitution.

convention: large meeting to present, discuss, and vote on issues.

discrimination: showing preference for one thing over another.

franchise: privilege or right, especially the right to vote.

grievance: complaint or expression of suffering.

legislature: group of officials that makes laws.

Quaker: person belonging to a Christian group that has no ministers, rejects church rituals, and opposes all wars and violence.

radical: very different or extreme.

ratify: formally approve something by voting on it.

reform: change in society designed to improve conditions.

reformer: person who campaigns for or introduces reforms.

repeal: undo a law that has been made earlier.

resolution: officially declared decision or intention.

revolution: huge change in belief or the way things are done.

sentiment: belief based on feelings or emotion.

subordination: keeping of one person at a lower level of rights or status so that another person can be superior and in charge.

suffrage: right to vote.

suffragette: woman who campaigned for women's rights, especially the right to vote.

temperance: moderation in something, especially in drinking alcohol.

textile: fabric that has been woven or knitted, such as wool and cotton.

U.S. territory: geographical area that belongs to and is governed by the United States but is not included in any of its states.

Further Information

Books
Bohannon, Lisa Frederiksen. *Women's Rights and Nothing Less: The Story of Elizabeth Cady Stanton.* Morgan Reynolds, 2001.
Keller, Kristin Thoennes. *The Women Suffrage Movement, 1848–1920.* Bridgestone, 2003.
Kendall, Martha E. *Susan B. Anthony: Voice for Women's Voting Rights (Historical American Biographies).* Enslow, 1997.
Sterling, Dorothy. *Lucretia Mott.* Feminist Press, 1999.
Wooldridge, Connie Nordhielm. *When Esther Morris Headed West: Women, Wyoming, and the Right to Vote.* Holiday House, 2001.

Web Sites
search.eb.com/women/index.html Information about women in American history from the Encyclopedia Britannica.
www.legacy98.org/ Historical account of the suffrage movement plus a time line and other resources from the National Women's History Project.
www.nps.gov/wori The National Park Service's web site offers information about and photographs of Women's Rights National Historical Park, together with historical information about the Seneca Falls Convention and the people who took part.
www.pbs.org/stantonanthony Information about the careers of Elizabeth Cady Stanton and Susan B. Anthony, taken from a documentary film.

Useful Addresses
Women's Rights National Historical Park
136 Fall Street
Seneca Falls, NY 13148
Telephone: (315) 568-2991

Index

Page numbers in **bold** indicate pictures.

abolition and abolitionists, 11, 12, 13, 17, **17**, 22
Anthony, Susan B., 22, 23, **23**

Bloomer, Amelia, **19**
Boston, 13

Catt, Carrie Chapman, 24

Declaration of Independence, 4–5, 6
"Declaration of Sentiments," 4, 5, 15, 17, 18, 19, 21, **21**, 25, 27
Dix, Dorothea, **8**
Douglass, Frederick, 17, **17**, 20

Equal Rights Association, 12

Hunt, Jane, 15, 26, **26**
Hunt, Richard, 17

Lowell Girls, 7, **7**
Lyon, Mary, 10

Massachusetts, **15**
M'Clintock, Mary Ann, 15, 18, 20
Mott, James, 12, 17, 18
Mott, Lucretia Coffin, 12, **12**, 13, 15, 19, 20, 25
Mount Holyoke College, 10

National American Woman Suffrage Association, 14
National Woman Suffrage Association, 14, 23
New York (state), 4, 14, **15**, 17
Nineteenth Amendment, 24, 25

Paul, Alice, 24
Philadelphia, 12, 13, **15**

reform and reformers, 8, **8**, 9, 10, 11, 12
Rice, Condoleezza, **27**

Seneca Falls, town of, 4, 14, **14**, **15**, 16, **16**, 26
Seneca Falls Women's Rights Convention, 4, 5, 12, 14, 15, 16–20, **18**, **20**, 21, 22, 25, 27
slavery, 11, **11**, 12
Stanton, Elizabeth Cady, 13, **13**, 14, 15, 17, 18, **18**, 19, 20, 21, 23, **23**, 25, 26
Stanton, Henry, 14, 17, 19
Stowe, Harriet Beecher, 11
suffrage, *see* women's rights
suffragettes, **4**, 24, **24**

temperance, 9, **9**, 11, 12

United States of America, 6, 26

Waterloo, 15, **15**, 26, **26**
Wesleyan Methodist Chapel, 15, 16, **16**, 26
women, position of, 5, 6–7, **7**, 8
women's rights, 4, 6, 13, 18, 20, 22, 23, 24, 26–27
  campaigners for, **4**, 5, 11, 12, **12**, 14, 15, 16, 17, 18, 19, 20, 21, 22, 23, **23**, 24, **24**, 25
  control of wages, 4, 22
  education, 4, 10, 18, 19, 22, 27
  equality in employment, 4, 6, 18, 20, 22, 27, **27**
  property, 4, 18, 22
  voting, 4, 5, **5**, 6, 17, 18, 19, 20, **22**, 23, 24, 25, **25**
Women's Rights National Historical Park, **14**, **21**, 26, **26**
Woodward, Charlotte, 16, 25
Wright, Martha Coffin, 15

MAY 1 4 2012
26-